DURHAM CITY
PAST AND PRESENT

DURHAM CITY
PAST AND PRESENT

MICHAEL RICHARDSON

breedon **books**
PUBLISHING

First published in Great Britain in 2007 by

The Breedon Books Publishing Company Limited

Breedon House, 3 The Parker Centre, Derby, DE21 4SZ.

To

Tommy and Spencer

ISBN 978-1-85983-581-4

Printed and bound by Cromwell Press, Trowbridge, Wiltshire

CONTENTS

ACKNOWLEDGMENTS

So many people have donated or loaned photographs, given time and advice, to the Gilesgate Archive that it would be impossible to thank them all individually. Special thanks go to: Kath Allison, Miss M. Almond, Frank Bilton, the late Miss C. Bramwell, Mr J.Campbell, Mr and Mrs N. Close, the late Donald Crampton, Major R.S. Cross, Walter Fenwick, Mr I. Forsyth, Julian Harrop, Tom Hay, Peter Jefferies, Dr Bob Kell, Ray Kitchen, Jim Lawson, the late George Lye, Miss D.M. Meade, the late Mr I. McIntyre, Mr G.R.S. Nelson, Roger Norris, Mr D. Pattison, Miss Emma Richardson, Mrs Norma Richardson, the late Joe Robinson, Mr E. Rolling, the late Dr John Salkeld, K. Salser, David Schofield, Canon John Spence, David Simpson, Carl Snowdon, Mark Summers and Dr John Yule.

The staff of the following institutions have helped in various ways: Clayport Library, Durham University Library, History of Durham Project, Beamish Museum, North of England Newspapers, *The Sunderland Echo* and Durham Record Office.

If you, the reader, have any old photographs, postcards, slides or negatives relating to the Durham City area and surrounding villages then the Gilesgate Archive would be delighted to hear from you. Whether you are lending or donating, all help is greatly appreciated.

'Preserving and Presenting The Past For The Future'

Please contact: gilesgatearchive@aol.com

Michael Richardson
c/o Gilesgate Archive
128 Gilesgate
Durham
DH1 1QG

FOREWORD

Like time machines, old photographs can carry us back to places we have long forgotten and even far beyond to times and places we never knew. Strangely compelling, they serve to remind us of our immortality and of the constant changes of time.

What a surprise to discover a familiar building in an unfamiliar setting, or an old-fashioned, long-forgotten shop façade where now there is only a chain store.

How exciting to find an old house or a friendly pub where now there is a roundabout or perhaps a shopping centre. How thrilling it is to study the happy faces of children in rags, or the whistling miners and men in cloth caps or the old-fashioned shopkeepers in their formal suits.

It might be argued that Durham City has seen little change compared with the larger towns and cities of our land. True, the cathedral and castle still dominate the skyline just as they did nine centuries ago, but they are the constants in a sea of change. Solidly rooted to their great rock and almost encircled by the River Wear, they serve as useful points of reference for photo detectives helping to identify forgotten photographed sites of the city.

Buildings, houses, old walls, and even streets, come and go with astonishing speed, and this has been very apparent in Durham. Without the medium of photography how soon we would forget them.

These changes have been no more dramatic than during the last decade or so. We have seen brand new streets sprouting up in the heart of the city like Highgate beneath the railway station and the so-called High Street of the new shopping centre. There is even a new town square, Millennium Square, on the fringe of the Market Place. It is a home to bars, restaurants, a cinema, a theatre and a library, where once there were only yards to the rear of Claypath.

Whether changes are applauded or widely despised they are an inevitable feature of local history in any town or city. This latest edition to Michael Richardson's outstanding library of Durham books presents us with the opportunity to compare and contrast the changes that have taken place in our wonderful city. Here we can compare images of Durham's past alongside the same scenes as they appear today. We may decide for ourselves what was good and what was bad, what is sadly missed and what has been improved for the better.

As with other works by Michael Richardson, *Durham City Past and Present* draws on decades of dedicated collecting and years of meticulous research. All of those who hold the beauty, atmosphere or memories of Durham City close to their hearts will enjoy this publication, and I wish Michael and his book every success.

David Simpson
The Northern Echo, North of England Newspapers, 2007.

INTRODUCTION

I am constantly being asked 'Where was this particular building?' or 'What did that shop used to be?' Sometimes it is difficult to explain the exact location without showing a recent photograph or having a map at hand. Therefore, I feel the time is right to introduce this before and after book, *Durham City Past and Present*.

There are six sections, broadly covering the areas: City Centre, North Road, New & Old Elvet, Crossgate, Claypath and Gilesgate. In the autumn of 2006 (October–November) I had great pleasure in walking around the city taking the recent photographs and explaining to people what my plans were for the new book.

Some of my personal favourites are: Mr James Watson, the knife-grinder at work on Elvet Bridge in 1924, the lamplighter in Waddington Street around 1911, the horse-drawn police van outside Durham railway station in the 1900s, sheep being driven up Crossgate in about 1938, and also the numerous old shopfronts long since vanished.

One of the biggest changes over the last 40 or so years has been the through road, which tore out property and gardens from the bottom of Gilesgate through to the lower end of Claypath in the 1960s. This was then thought to be the answer to Durham's traffic problem. The demolition between the 1930s and 1960s produced numerous pleasant open green areas. Unfortunately, over the last 10 years or so, most of these have been sold as sites, mainly for private housing. We have lost at least four children's play areas in Gilesgate alone during the last 15 years for redevelopment, one of the oldest being the 'duff heap', which had been created by the city council from the former Kepier colliery waste heap in around 1929.

On the brighter side we now have a new shopping area, High Street, and the Millennium Square with its library, cinema, theatre and restaurant-bars. Despite many changes, Durham still retains the old mediaeval small-town character, with its hidden lanes and vennels, pleasant riverside walks and warm friendly atmosphere. Above it loom the Norman cathedral and castle (designated a World Heritage Site in 1987 by UNESCO), built on rock and surrounded by the horseshoe loop of the River Wear.

Since the archive was formed some 20 years ago, photographs have arrived from around the world, most of which have been unique and would have been lost forever had it not been for the Gilesgate Archive. I would like to take this opportunity to thank all of those who have loaned or donated them. As a result many people of Durham (and further afield) have enjoyed viewing lost images of bygone Durham. I hope that this volume will bring the reader as much pleasure as it has given me in putting it together.

Michael Richardson, 2007.

CITY CENTRE AREA

Durham Cathedral and Fulling Mill from South Street Mill, *c*.1875, photographed by Thomas Heaviside. The man in the photograph is said to be Heaviside himself; with the lengthy exposure time needed, it was possible for him to set up the camera and pose for the shot. This is probably the most famous view of Durham, known worldwide.

The Londonderry monument, Durham Market Place, c.1925. It was the work of Raffaelle Monti and was unveiled on 2 December 1861 in the presence of Benjamin Disraeli. The electro-plated copper statue had been commissioned by Francis Anne, Lady Londonderry, at a cost of £2,000 paid in advance. Before it was delivered Monti went bankrupt, and the sculpture was seized by his creditors. Lady Londonderry had to pay a further £1,000 before it was handed over. The base was erected by a local mason, Mr T. Winter. The statue was taken down and restored in 1952.

Durham Market Place, 1870s. On the left is part of the town hall, constructed between 1849–51, to the designs of Philip Charles Hardwick, at the same time the old guildhall was restored and doubled in size in a gothic style. St Nicholas' Church on the right was rebuilt in 1857–58 by J.P. Pritchett on the foundations of an earlier church. At this time there was no statue (of the patron saint) in the niche above the church door.

An inside view of St Nicholas' Church, Market Place, looking east. It was photographed prior to the re-ordering in the 1970s by the then vicar, the Revd George Carey (later Archbishop of Canterbury). Note the World War One memorial on the south wall, left of the doorway on the right, which was designed by a parishioner, W.G. Footitt. This church is probably the only church in the city (apart from the cathedral) that is open seven days a week.

The Market Hotel and New Markets entrance, 1919. The notice in the hotel window reads 'No Ladies Supplied', an indication of the firm stance against women drinkers made by some establishments at that period. It was here on 20 November 1869 that the Durham Miners' Association was formed in a back meeting room.

The stall of Hayton's novelty bazaar, Durham Indoor Market, *c.*1909, situated on the left-hand side. The interior has been described as being of slender Tuscan cast-iron columns supporting pierced beams and tied trusses with a glazed roof. The photograph (issued as a postcard) had been sent to Eleanor from Polly, of 22 Gilesgate, cancelling a visit to the Palace Theatre.

The Rose and Crown Hotel, decorated for the Diamond Jubilee of Queen Victoria, 1897. The proprietor, William MacFarlane, and his staff, can be seen on the left. Note the spectator, right of the central flag-pole on the roof-top. The premises ceased to be licensed in March 1928 and later became Woolworth's store, prior to the present purpose-built shop.

The bank of J. Backhouse and Company, Market Place (now Barclay's Bank), built by the leading architect Alfred Waterhouse in 1887 (his masterpiece was the magnificent Manchester Town Hall). On its right is Sarsfield the chemist (with the Bowes Arms Hotel above) and, far right, Procter the printer, 1890s. The property was demolished about 1923 to make way for the 1924 extension to the bank. The lead statue of Neptune is seen on the right, on its second pant head, erected in 1863. This was later replaced by a domed pant head in 1902, which survived until December 1923. It was then placed in Wharton Park, until being restored (1986) and brought back to the Market Place in 1991.

The *Evening Chronicle* office, Market Place, 1950s. The man wearing the light coat in the doorway is reporter Mr C.F. Close of Gilesgate. The building had previously been Procter's printing and stationery shop (now City Sports).

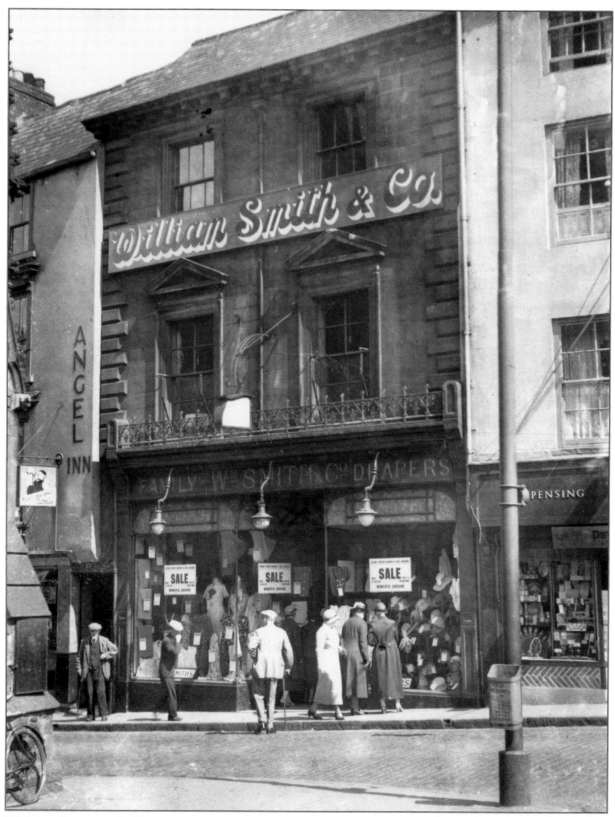

The shopfrontage of William Smith and Company, general and soft furnishing drapers, Market Place, 1930s. Signs in the window indicate a sale of goods. Far left is the Angel Inn public house, and right is part of Taylor's the chemist. The site is now next to the Market Place entrance to the Prince Bishops' shopping centre. The decorative stone work on the left is part of St Nicholas' Church.

Saddler Street from the Market Place, 1940s. The old photograph shows, left to right: Hiller's music shop, H.M. Coyne, draper, House of Andrews bookshop, Rushworth and Storey, fruiterers (previously Lockey's, see p.21), Dermont's newsagent and stationer, the London Lending Library and R. Dixon, butcher. This section of the street was once called Fleshergate, it being the area occupied by the butchers.

The shopfront of Hepworth's gentlemen's outfitters, Saddler Street, 6 September 1918, photographed by Mr Stafford for the Speedy Photo Company, Durham. It shows The Dunelm Window Cleaners: left to right; Mrs R. Marshall, Miss W. Burke and Mr H.G. Marshall. During World War One, the shortage of manpower meant many women were called upon to do work previously carried out only by men. The building was later demolished and a branch of the HSBC Bank now occupies the site.

F. Lockey's Supply Stores and Café, 76 Saddler Street, *c*.1909. The decorative panel covering the first-floor window shows an Indian and Chinaman advertising their fine teas. The Lockey family lived in Rossleigh House, Bede Bank, now occupied by the Principal of Hild-Bede College. The shop is currently a branch of the Northern Rock Building Society.

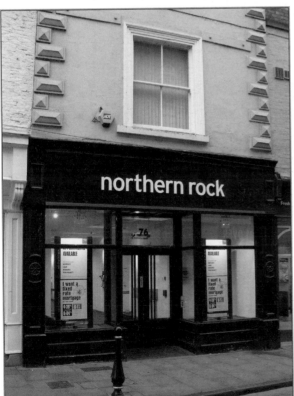

Book's (Fashion) Ltd, 71 Saddler Street, 1956, showing its unsightly signage. It had previously been Hiller's music shop. The premises are now a branch of the Edinburgh Woollen Mill. The present frontage is more in keeping with the building.

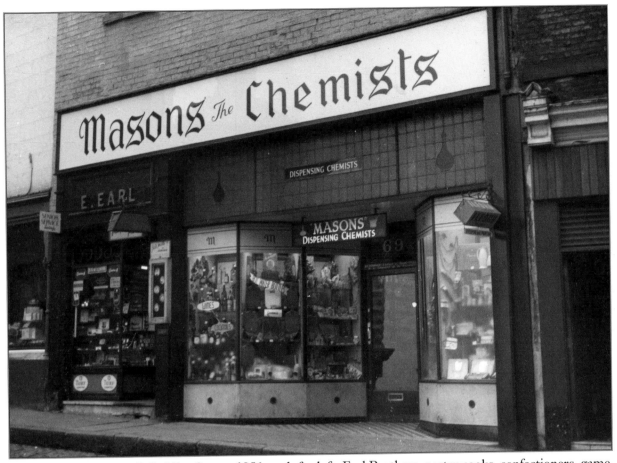

Masons the Chemist, 69 Saddler Street, 1956, and, far left, Earl Brothers, pastry cooks, confectioners, game & poultry dealers, and, between the two shops, E. Earl, tobacconist. The tobacconist is now incorporated into Waterstone's bookshop. The present shopfront has been carefully designed to blend in with the surrounding property.

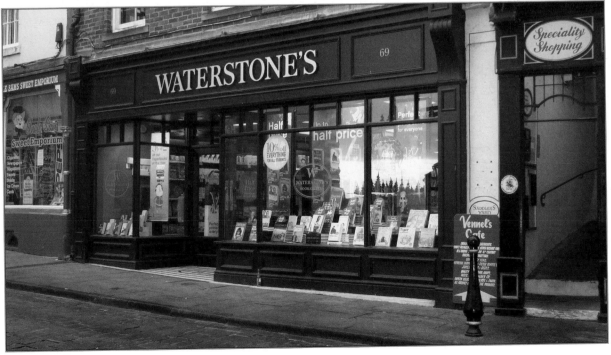

The junction of Saddler Street and Elvet Bridge from Fleshergate (now part of Saddler Street), *c*.1860. In the centre is the area once known as 'Bailes Corner'. The premises were those of the Bailes brothers, shoe & boot makers (cordwainers). The building was compulsorily purchased by the Local Board of Health for £1,250 to make way for road improvements, and it was removed in June 1864. The site is now occupied by the Magdalene Steps.

Maynard's confectionery shop, 8 Saddler Street, with its special window display for the Miners' Gala, 1929.
The girl on the right is Grace Adams. In later years crowds at the Gala were so large that shopkeepers placed
boards over their windows to prevent people being pressed against the glass in the narrow mediaeval streets.
The shop now belongs to Alastair Wade, optician.

The shop window of the Eclipse Wallpaper Co., 9 Saddler Street, *c.*1929. Many people will remember having to cut the borders from the rolls of wallpaper. The shop on the left was Maynards (see p.25). The premises are now a kitchenware shop called La Cookshop, opposite the Magdalene Steps.

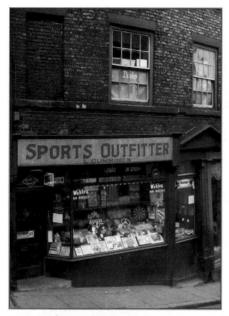

The shop of L. Cummings, sports outfitter, Elvet Bridge, 1956. Note the blocked-up first-floor window above the door and the advertisements in the window for Webley air rifles and pistols. The shop was very popular, selling a wide range of sporting goods from ice-skates to shotguns. It is now occupied by Strides menswear.

Mr James Watson, knife-grinder, at work outside the City Fish and Game Company, 17 Elvet Bridge, May 1924, photographed by W.A. Bramwell. At the time of the photograph Mr Watson, of Framwellgate, had been sharpening knives and scissors in the city for 50 years. He had followed his father and grandfather in the trade. The shop had previously belonged to Samuel Hume, jeweller and watchmaker. The shop on the left was Pattisons, upholsterers, and the building on the right was the telephone exchange. The fish and game shop is now a bar and restaurant called Hollathan's.

Fillingham's photography shop, 12 Elvet Bridge, *c.*1938. George Fillingham, a native of Peterborough, was for a time an auctioneer in Yorkshire before coming to Durham as the manager of the Science and Art Studio, 69 Saddler Street. He later opened his own business on Elvet Bridge, which flourished long after his death in November 1931. The business was inherited by Mr George Lye and finally closed in 2000. Since the recent photograph of 'Bear Bottoms' teddy-bear shop (October 2006), the premises have now been taken over by Oxfam.

Dimambro's ice-cream and confectionary shop, Elvet Bridge, *c.*1930. The advertisements on the shopfront include those for Fry's and Cadbury's chocolate, gold flake and capstan tobacco products. Showing: left, Tommy Martin and, right, Andrew Dimambro. The building on the right was Miss Campbell's ladies' and children's outfitter. Dimambro's is now occupied by a fashion clothes shop called Van Mildert. The doorway on the right (recent photograph) leads to Jimmy Allen's bar, which is partly situated under the bridge in the old house of correction (a former gaol).

Riverside House, Elvet Bridge, 1920s. The building stood behind Brown's boat house on the west side near the old house of correction, located under the archway on the right of the steps. The area is now a pleasant paved open space.

Brown's boathouse, Elvet Bridge, 1911, showing preparations for the launch of the pleasure boat *The Dunelm*, built by Joseph Brown. Caldcleugh's printing works can be seen to the left of the boathouse behind the bridge. The boathouse was almost demolished several years ago, but it has been given a new lease of life having been converted into a popular watering-hole called The Chase.

Looking towards Fleshergate from near the Magdalene Steps, Saddler Street, late 1950s. Note the student in his academic gown, then a common sight in the city, before the present more relaxed dress code was allowed. The United Shoe Shop and its neighbour on the left have been replaced by one of the entrances to the Prince Bishops' shopping centre.

The Victory Café & confectioners, 36 Saddler Street, March 1938, run by brother and sister Harry and Jenny Walton. A Scottie dog stands guard over the pram and its occupant, with a snarl like Gnasher from the *Beano* comic book. The recent photograph shows the ornate Victorian wooden shopfront. On the gable (not on the photograph) are carved the initials TM and the date 1844. A later date, 1979, records the time when some restoration work was carried out. It is now occupied by Saddlers, Coffee Bar and Bistro.

Looking down Saddler Street from near the Salvation Army Citadel, 1960s. On the left is the Buffalo Head public house, now renamed the Hog's Head. The spire in the background is that of St Nicholas' Church, which is having work carried out on it by a steeplejack. This stretch of the road leading to the cathedral is now controlled by Britain's first road toll. It is free to enter but costs £2 to exit, operating six days a week 10am to 4pm.

The Edis photography studio, 52 Saddler Street, 1920s, showing some of their fine photographs of the cathedral in the shop window. The business had been started by John Edis in the 1890s. After his death in 1942, it was continued by his daughter Daisy and finally closed in the early 1960s. It is now occupied by the Georgian Window, gift shop.

The west side of Palace Green, showing a lone university policeman, *c*.1900. On the left is Palace Green library, built by Sir Arthur William Blomfield (1829–99), dating from 1882. The central building with the turret window is Bishop Cosin's library, founded in 1669 (restored in 1798) for clergy of the diocese and built by architect John Longstaffe. On the right is the 15th-century exchequer and chancery (Palatinate Courts). This area is part of the World Heritage Site.

Looking along the North Bailey, 1900s, towards St Mary-le-Bow, a mediaeval church, the rebuilding of which began *c.*1685 (note the fine cobbled street). The old cottage and coach houses on the right of the church were pulled down to make way for St Chad's dining hall in 1961. In the centre of the old photograph, at the bottom of Dun Cow Lane, is the former Castle Inn. Durham Freemasons' lodge met there from 1768–81.

The Durham County war memorial, North Bailey, 24 November 1928. This rare photograph captures the precise moment that the curtain falls, unveiling the memorial dedicated to those who lost their lives in World War One. To the left is the Lord Lieutenant of the County, the Marquess of Londonderry. The sculpture was designed by Professor C.H. Reilly of Liverpool University and executed by Mr H. Tyson of Liverpool. When finished it was brought to Durham and erected by local builders Frank Goodyear & Son. The recent photograph shows the wooden fence which has hidden the memorial for many years due to restoration work being carried out on the east end of the cathedral.

St Mary-the-Less, South Bailey; an engraving by William Pearson, *c.*1831. The 12th-century church was rebuilt in 1846–47 by George Pickering, incorporating some of the original material. On the left is the former priest's house, later used as a garage and now converted to a quiet study area for students of St John's College. The church is used as a chapel by St John's.

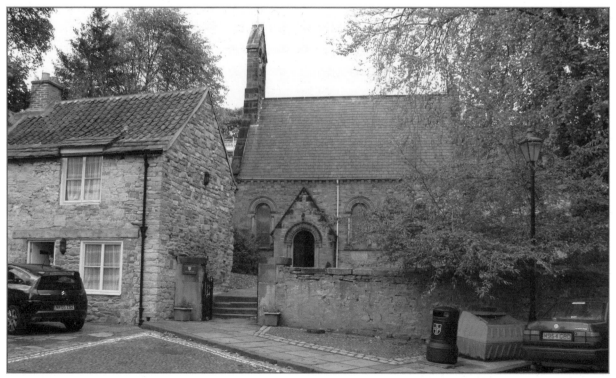

Watergate, South Bailey, from the cathedral banks, 1900s. The original postern gate stood a little to the east of the present gateway. The stone arch shown was erected in 1778 by Canon Henry Egerton to allow carriages to enter the Bailey from the newly-built Prebends Bridge. The old building through the archway was later demolished and replaced by the new junior common room of St Cuthberts Society in the early 1960s.

The 'Counts House', near Prebends Bridge, built around 1810 in the Greek Doric style, pictured *c.*1914. At the time of the postcard teas were sold here at weekends and holidays. The house was then lived in by the Lee family, whose daughter Eva is pictured at the gate. This area was known as 'Count's Corner' after the famed Polish dwarf, Count Joseph Boruwlaski (1739–1837). He had in the later part of his life lodged with the Ebdon family in a large property nearby, long since demolished. This summer house belonged to a house in the Bailey and is commonly called 'Count's House'. It is listed on the Ordnance Survey Map of 1857 as Shipperdson's cottage.

The path below the steps at the foot of Silver Street leading to the Fulling Mill ('the bottom trod'), *c.*1906, photographed by George Fillingham. This area was extensively landscaped with the planting of native trees, shrubs, new paths and seating between 1875–76, under the direction of Canon H.B. Tristram.

The ornate shopfront belonging to Ramsbottoms, pork butcher, 19 Silver Street, 1920s. The steps and handrail on the right lead to the riverside footpath (above) and Fulling Mill. The sign partially seen on the left is for the Castle Hotel, which was next door. The premises were for many years occupied by Dunn and Company gentlemen's outfitter. It is now a mobile phone shop.

Looking up Silver Street, *c*.1965. Until the mid-1970s traffic was still using this narrow, mediaeval street. Some readers will remember the occasional knock by vehicle wing-mirrors. The bus shown is a United Bristol 'LS' type, serving Durham to Peterlee. The street is now pedestrianised.

Boots Cash Chemist, 29 Silver Street, 1947. Left to right: Elsie Chapman, Jean Appleby, Doris Young, Rita Bland, Marion Batey and Laura Milne. The reflection in the left window shows the name of Dewhurst the butcher, whose shop was immediately opposite. The chemist is now a discount bookshop and stationer called The Works.

Old property at the bottom of Silver Street below the castle walls, viewed from the steps on the north side of Framwellgate Bridge, 1890s. The single-storey cottage adjoining the footpaths on the middle right of the old photograph is now a small courtyard used by a neighbouring coffee shop. The buildings in the foreground were demolished in the 1960s – a pizza restaurant with offices above now occupy the site.

Framwellgate Bridge, showing a Gillett and Baker bus of Quarrington Hill, *c.*1946. This is a posed photograph for the company, as the bus did not run on this route. The business was started by the three Gillett brothers in 1922, with a Ford Model T, seating 14 passengers. They were later joined by J.J. Baker, who had also started off in the 1920s. This partnership finished in October 1959, when the Baker side of the business ceased and their garage was absorbed into the Gillett concern. The name of the company was then changed from Gillett and Baker to G.B. Gillett Brothers (Motor Services) Ltd.

Lambton Walk from Silver Street, 1960s. The ground floors of these properties were often flooded, therefore most of the occupants kept their good furniture on the first floor. The area is now part of Millburngate (The Gates) shopping centre. Even today the problem of flooding still exists. On the extreme left can be seen the site of the old Criterion Hotel, prior to the building of the Coach and Eight public house.

NORTH ROAD AREA

Looking towards North Road from Framwellgate Bridge on a busy day, 1920s. On the left is the old Criterion public house. The central building belonged to F.G. Pennington, grocer, later occupied by S. Hume, jeweller (see p.56). The premises on the right are: The Public Benefit Boot and Shoe Company Ltd, S. Smith, cycle agent, and M.A. McLean, ladies' outfitter. The ground floor of the latter premises is now one of the entrances to Millburngate shopping centre.

Looking towards the bottom of South Street from Millburngate, 1950s; South Street addresses start at the end of Framwellgate Bridge. On the extreme right is the Fighting Cocks public house. The property to its left was later demolished and replaced by a featureless 1960s building. On the far left of the photograph is Miss M. Reece's confectionary shop, and to its right is the Five Ways Inn public house (closed in 1966).

John Oliver, fish, game and poultry dealer, 131 Millburngate, *c.*1950. Note the telephone number 82, the chalk board advertising Craster kippers and the notice 'Please order early for Xmas'. The shop's name continued as that of a general dealer, at Hawthorn Terrace, until 2006. The Millburngate shop is now 'Chaps' barber's.

Looking down Millburngate, showing, on the right, the Five Ways Inn, *c.*1966. Its name derived from the roads leading to it: Millburngate, North Road, South Street, Crossgate and Framwellgate Bridge. On the far left of the row is Stanton's fish and chip shop and next door to it is Miss M.Reece's confectionary shop. In the distance can be seen the construction of the new Millburngate Bridge and beyond that the former ice-skating rink.

Looking towards Millburngate from Framwellgate in the late 1960s. The building to the left belonged to Blagdon's leather works. This was the last property to be demolished prior to the building of phase one of Millburngate shopping centre, the foundation stone being laid in March 1974. The old photograph shows the new road layout under construction.

A view of Durham Castle, Cathedral and Framwellgate Bridge from Millburngate, 1870s, taken by Thomas Heaviside. The bridge was built *c.*1120 by Bishop Flambard. On the far left is the dry arch said to be from the original bridge, now hidden by a modern building. In 1401 this structure was rebuilt by Bishop Langley after being damaged by flood. The local Board of Health passed a motion on 6 July 1859 for the bridge to be improved and widened.

The King William IV public house (closed 1966), North Road, *c.*1966. One of the oak doors from the front of the pub was salvaged by Mrs Watson of Kepier Farm and is now the main front door of the farm house. On the left was Lawson's newsagents. The area is now occupied by an oriental gift shop, the Abbey National Building Society, a shoe shop and a taxi rank.

The premises of Samuel Hume, jeweller, 1 North Road, *c.*1923. On the left is Walter Holdsworth (owner), and on the right is George R. Middlemass (clock and watch repairer). The business had been started by Walter's father-in-law, S. Hume, around 1861 in Gilesgate. It later moved to King Street (North Road), then Atherton Street, followed by Elvet Bridge, and finally back to North Road. Note on the extreme left of the older photograph part of Gleason's tinsmith's shop (see p.120).

John Oliver (standing in the doorway), poultry dealer, 2 North Road, 1920s, photographed by Ernest, Silver Street, near Christmas with all the birds prepared and hanging on the front of the building. For many years it was the Army and Navy Stores and, later, Greenwell's delicatessen for a short time before being redeveloped. The site is now occupied by Specsavers and Greggs bakery.

Jagal (from the first letters of the following: J. and G. Archibald Limited) House, Archibald's Store, North Road, 1962. The building was designed by Cordingley and McIntyre and built by Holst and Company Limited (opened 29 February 1956). The premises are now demolished and have been redeveloped. Today they are occupied by several retail premises.

Palmer's Temperance hotel and café, 4 North Road, 1900s, then run by the Palmer sisters, Ann and Sarah. The old building was demolished several years ago, and the present building was built in the same style. Today, Burger King fast food chain occupies the ground floor and above is an Indian restaurant.

The Jubilee Methodist Church, North Road, c.1961. It was opened on 19 May 1861. The congregation had previously been meeting in a little chapel in Back Silver Street. The North Road building is now demolished and was replaced by a building destitute of distinct features, occupied by Iceland freezer store.

Durham Miners' Gala procession, North Road, 1890s. The procession consists of a mounted band of guardsmen. The premises on the left are: Adamson and Company, painters, G. Turner, furniture dealer, Dermont's, Shadforth, auctioneer and cabinet-maker. Far right is the old Durham Miners' Hall, erected 1874–75.

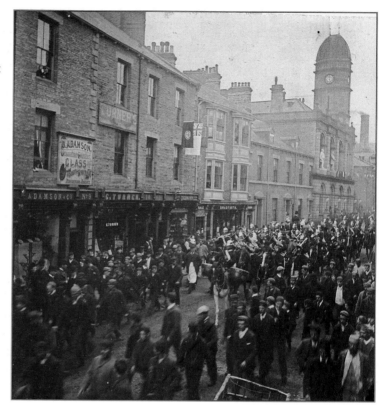

Durham Miners' Gala procession, North Road, 1890s, showing the only known photograph of this particular banner from Cornsay Colliery. The procession is passing the Singer sewing machine shop and the archway entrance to Pounder's City Saleroom. Note the train passing over the viaduct. The property on the right of the old photograph is now occupied by modern business premises, built *c.*1974, one of which is now Yates' Wine Lodge.

Staddon's toy shop, North Road, early 1970s. The firm continued until the mid-1980s. The size of the shop windows filled with goods is an indication of its popularity and patronage by local citizens. Three separate businesses now occupy the former premises.

The Essoldo Cinema, North Road, 1950s. Built by local builder George Gradon of North Road, it was previously called the Regal when it was opened in March 1934. The old cinema is now an Australian theme bar called Walkabout. The centre building is the old Miners' Hall. Next door to it is the entrance to the premises of J.W. Wood, auctioneer. On the far right is the old Neville Hotel, rebuilt in the early 1960s, now named Bar 19.

Durham bus station, North Road, *c.*1926. The building on the right was the City Mill, a flour mill belonging to R.V. Hills. This was demolished shortly after the photograph was taken and the new cast-iron bus station was erected. In turn the buildings were taken down for the present nondescript building erected in the 1970s. The recent photograph shows the former Avenue Temperance Hotel, later used as the canteen for the United Bus Company. This fine Georgian villa dates from about 1842 and was built by J.L. Pearson, the Durham architect (his first recorded work).

A United bus with the destination panel showing Sherburn Village, standing near the railway viaduct, 1960s. The area is north of the new roundabout at the top of North Road. The businesses on the left are Macrae's, draper, and R. Middleton's, grocer. Opposite the shop is the Station Hotel. All of the properties were lost when the new road was constructed.

The Station Hotel, North Road, before this area was cleared for the new road scheme, late 1960s. Note the viaduct, top left of the old photograph, and, on the right, the Victorian town houses of North Road, also demolished for the new road scheme. The site is now occupied by a pleasant tree-covered slope.

Looking down North Road from near the viaduct, 1950s. On the right is Bramwell's the newsagent and further down, to the right of the lamp-post, is the Bethel Chapel, built in the classical style by E.R. Robson. The foundation stone was laid in 1853 and it opened the following year. On the left side of the road is the old Globe cinema (opened May 1913), now occupied by a hairdressing and beauty salon, with a restaurant above.

The Bridge Hotel (wine and spirit merchants), North Road, 1900s. The hotel was established about 1864. At the time of the photograph, it was managed by Edwin Alfred Oliver, who was there from 1897–1926. The hotel now has the neigbouring property on the left as a dining area. The top left of the photograph shows part of the railway viaduct.

Waddington Street, *c.*1911, showing the lamplighter at work, possibly changing the gas–mantle. The street was named after Dean George Waddington (died July 1869). He was the prime mover in the founding of the Durham County Hospital. The building on the end of the terrace belonged to the South Durham Tea Company. It had previously been Ainsley's printing works & mustard mill.

Looking down Albert Street, Western Hill (built between the 1850s and 60s), *c*.1910, photographed by George Fillingham. It is one of the few unchanged streets in the city. Most of the houses still retain their original iron railings to the front of the properties. These were exempt from the salvaging of iron during World War Two as they protected pedestrians from falling into the basement area.

Field House, Albert Street, Western Hill, 1900s, showing the Robinson children. Their father, William, is listed at this time in the *Durham City Directory* as working for the railway. This house had no basement; therefore, it was safe to remove the railings for the war effort.

Durham Light Infantry cottage homes, Western Hill, *c.*1903. In 1902 the land was purchased and two cottages were built. The first was a memorial to HH Prince Christian Victor of Schleswig-Holstein. He was Queen Victoria's grandson and died of fever in Pretoria, while serving with the King's Royal Rifles in the Boer War. The second was dedicated to the memory of the officers and men of the Durham Light Infantry who lost their lives in the South African War. The first occupants were Privates Coulthard and Norwood, who had been wounded at Val Krantz.

A horse-drawn police van outside the south entrance of Durham Railway Station, 1900s, photographed by W. Wilkinson. This was used to transport prisoners to and from the prison in Old Elvet. It was a common sight at the time to see children following it through the town chanting rhymes.

Durham from the battery, Wharton Park, 1930s. The cannon and gun were taken away for the war effort during World War Two (August 1940). Note the flag pole. The battery was built about the same time as the railway viaduct, c.1856, by W.L. Wharton of Dryburn Hall. He probably took advantage of the surplus stone and manpower just a few hundred yards away.

'Wharton Park Sports', an event held in the park, 1890s. The stone structure in the background is part of the old pavilion (see p.76). Sports were a regular feature in the park, first encouraged by John Lloyd Wharton (nephew of W.L. Wharton of Dryburn Hall), who was a keen high jumper himself. The park was named after the Wharton family and was leased to the City Corporation for 99 years. In 1913 the city became absolute owner. The area is now occupied by a dodgem car-track for small children, a conservatory and, in the distance, tennis courts.

The Durham Shakespeare Temperance Band at 'The Rink' (roller-skating), Wharton Park, c.1936. The rink area is now known as the pavilion. Front row, left, is Mr Harold Mollon. The park is one of Durham's treasures, hidden on a hill behind the railway station.

Millburngate from Framwellgate Bridge, 1960s, showing the new Millburngate House and bridge during construction. The land on the left was an open-air car park prior to the building of Millburngate shopping centre. The area, once heavily populated, was cleared in the 1920s and 30s as part of a slum clearance scheme, most of the families being moved up to a new housing estate on Sherburn Road.

The Tanners' Arms public house, 48 Framwellgate, 1950s. It stood on the north side of the road below the railway embankment at the head of Framwellgate. It was still lit inside by gas until it closed. The site is now occupied by luxury town houses and apartments.

The old Three Horse Shoes, 64 Framwellgate, *c.*1959. The pub stood at the head of Framwellgate on the right-hand side of the road near the railway bridge. Note the blocked-up window above the door, painted to look like a Georgian-style window. In the foreground is the Fram Well head, which was recorded as far back as 1450. A new well-head (the one in the photograph) was built in 1847. This was restored and moved across the road to the site of the former public house in about 1959.

Durham from Sidegate, 1920s. The chimney on the right belonged to the old Sidegate Colliery, and the centre fenced area later became Holiday Park dog-track, named after the owner, Thomas Holiday. The view is now obscured by the building of a new hotel.

The Schofield family outside Crook Hall farm house, Sidegate, *c.*1909, showing Elizabeth and Henry with their children, William (left) and Jane. Note the wooden block to the left of the door, used for chopping sticks. The present house has been altered and extended, retaining lots of original features. Standing outside on the recent photograph is the present owner, George O'Donnell.

NEW AND OLD ELVET AREA

Elvet Bridge from Fearon's Walk, 1890s. The walk, stretching from Elvet Bridge to Hatfield boathouse, constructed in 1883, was provided for public use through the efforts of the Reverend William Andrewes Fearon DD, headmaster of Durham School. Unfortunately a new sign has been erected on the east side of the bridge calling it 'Riverside Walk', despite the original bronze plaque, on a wall west of the bridge, calling it Fearon's Walk. The building left of the dry arch occupied the site of St Andrew's Chantry Chapel, established in the late 13th century.

Elvet Bridge, looking towards Saddler Street, early 1970s, showing the busy traffic prior to it being pedestrianised in 1975. The bridge was built, c.1160, by Bishop Hugh of Le Puiset. It was partly destroyed in the great flood of 1771 and was rebuilt in the same style. In 1804–05 it was doubled in width.

Durham City Workmen's Club, 2 Old Elvet, *c.*1904. It had formerly been known by several names: The Wheatsheaf Inn, The Royal Mail Inn, The Cycle Hotel and, finally, the Workmen's Club. The old gas lamp has, painted on three sides, 'Durham Workmen's Club'. The building was later demolished and is now occupied by four small retail shops, three of which still have their decorative mosaic-tiled entrances. (The mosiacs were made by Lowes' Marble Works of Gilesgate.)

Miss Emma Jarvis outside her tobacconist shop, 2 Old Elvet, June 1911. The premises were decorated for the Coronation of King George V and Queen Mary. One of the advertisements on the shopfront is for 'Wills Gold Flake cigarettes 10 for 3d'. The premises are now part of the Oddbins off-licence chain. Regrettably, the mosaic-tiled entrance has been covered with modern quarry tiles.

A military parade by the Marquess of Londonderry's 2nd Durham Artillery Volunteers, Old Elvet, 1890s. The large building on the left was demolished about 1902 to create access for the new Wesleyan Methodist Church. Note, on the old photograph, the open window in the attic gable, probably the maids' quarters.

The Waterloo Hotel, 61 Old Elvet, *c.*1966. It was located between the old County Court Offices and the Royal County Hotel and was taken down to make way for the approach to the New Elvet road bridge, which was built in 1975 and opened to traffic a year later. Before the bridge was erected, all traffic would have to travel over the ancient Elvet Bridge and through the Market Place.

Looking down Old Elvet, 1950s. This is one of the few streets to have changed very little over the last 100 years. The 'sentry box' on the right was for the car parking attendant to shelter from the weather. The wall to the right of the centre car was later taken down for an access road to Elvet Waterside. Notice, in the distance, the steep incline of Elvet Bridge.

Durham's newly-built swimming baths, 1932. They were opened that year by Lord Barnard at a cost of £31,519 and replaced the earlier baths of 1855. The main contractor was G.W. Lazenby and Company Limited of Ferryhill. Note the stone piers of the old iron bridge on the left and, right, an old cottage with wooden, ground-floor window shutters. The site of the latter is now occupied by a car park.

The first Baths Bridge (officially called Pelaw Leazes Bridge), *c.*1875. It was constructed from wood and opened in 1855. This bridge was later replaced by an iron construction in about 1894–96. This, in turn, was taken down and the present reinforced concrete one was opened on 16 June 1962 by Councillor J.O. Luke. Behind is Woodbine Cottage (see p.208), a fine Georgian building, now demolished.

An early photograph of Durham Regatta showing in the background the open-top grandstand on The Racecourse, 1890s. The horse races dated as far back as 1665 and continued until about 1887. The stone from the grandstand was salvaged and re-used by a local builder for the frontage of Mountjoy Crescent, Elvet (see article in *The Durham County Advertiser*, 10 June 1932).

Mr and Mrs Haswell outside their lodging house, 38 Old Elvet, *c.*1908. The accommodation was described on the back of the original postcard as being quaint, quiet with convenient postal facilities (note the pillar-box). The property is next door to the Dun Cow public house. This 18-roomed building was on the market on behalf of the owners, Durham University, for offers in the region of £600,000 (October 2006).

Looking down from the head of Old Elvet, 1900s, photographed by the Science and Art Company, Saddler Street. The cast-iron balcony, centre right, behind the lamp-post, was said to be specially erected as a viewing-point when the public hangings took place in the 1800s. The last public hanging was 10 March 1865, when Matthew Atkinson was hanged for the murder of his wife near Winlaton. On the first attempt the rope broke, but a second attempt 30 minutes later completed the job.

Elvet Railway Station at the head of Old Elvet, 1900s. The station had opened in 1893 and had a short life as a passenger line, closing in January 1931. It continued as a goods line and was used each July to bring miners and their families in for the Durham Miners' Gala until 1953. It had been sold to Durham County Council in 1949 and was demolished in 1963. The station site is now occupied by Durham Magistrates' Court.

The railway signal-box, belonging to Elvet Station, 1940s. The area is now part of the staff car park for the tax office in Green Lane. The buildings on the right are the former railway employees' cottages. Between the lamp-post and the signal-box can be seen (in the distance) the newly-built chapel in the grounds of Bede College.

Elvet railway bridge looking towards Old Durham Gardens, *c.*1933. It spanned the river between Old Durham and Hollow Drift. Constructed *c.*1892 by T.D. Ridley of Middlesbrough, the iron work was carried out by the Stockton Forge. Under the arch of the bridge, in the distance, are the gazebo and walled garden at Old Durham. The bridge was taken down in the 1960s; all that remains are the brick abutments.

Looking down New Elvet towards the old County Court Offices, 1966. Archaeological digs, prior to the building of Elvet Riverside lecture rooms (off the left of the photograph), unearthed the remains of early mediaeval dwellings. The spire in the distance is that of the United Reformed Church in Claypath.

The Cock Tavern, New Elvet, 1880s. This building was typical of the style that lined the city streets in the 17th century. Note the heavy stone roof slabs, horizontal-sliding sash windows, wooden shutters and upper blocked window. The property no longer survives, the site now being occupied by a modern extension to the right of the Three Tuns Hotel car park.

Looking across the river from Fearon's Walk, towards the newly-built Hatfield View council houses, New Elvet, *c.*1929 (named after their view of Hatfield College on the opposite side of the river). Some of the residents are watching a regatta race. The area is now occupied by unsightly university offices and an open space between Elvet Riverside lecture rooms and Dunelm House.

The car belonging to the Chief Constable, Sir George Morley, at the rear of the old police station, Court Lane, March 1926, photographed by John Edis. The spire in the background belongs to Elvet Methodist Church. The recent photograph shows the present police car park of the new station situated in New Elvet.

Looking down Court Lane, New Elvet, 1920s, originally called 'Ratton [or Rotten] Row'. The buildings at the bottom left of the lane were later taken down to make way for shops as part of the New Elvet slum clearance. On the extreme left, under construction, are the council houses of Court Lane. The new police station car park and Orchard House apartments for the over 50s now occupy the site of the property on the right side of the old photograph.

The old Hare and Hounds Hotel, 54 New Elvet, c.1905. About 1961, when the hotel was being demolished, a seam of coal was rediscovered in the cellar. For several nights afterwards cars were seen, with their back-ends loaded down, leaving the site. An open area between Dunelm House and Elvet Riverside lecture rooms now occupies the site.

Old properties on the east side of New Elvet, 1907, from a watercolour by F.A.Phipson. These old buildings were taken down in the late 1920s and replaced with smart retail shops. Note the barber's pole on the left building. To the right of the shops on the recent photograph is the entrance to Elvet Crescent council houses.

Looking down from the top of New Elvet, *c.*1900. Most of the properties, apart from the row of shops on the right of the recent photograph, vanished in the 1950s and early 1960s. The university building, Dunelm House, now occupies the site just off on the left-hand side of the photograph (see p.104).

The mock-Tudor shopfront of Clarke's Library Book Company, 28 New Elvet, *c.*1931, belonging to George Gibb Clarke, FLA. Left to right: Karl Adamson, unknown, Mrs E. Clarke and Jane Dixon Slack. Note the sign above Mr Adamson, which reads 'You may telephone from here'. The business later moved up to North Road. The Elvet premises are now a branch of Lloyds Bank.

Church Lane, looking towards St Oswald's vicarage and the central tower of the cathedral, Church Street, July 1938. The cobbled lane linked up with Hallgarth Street. Among the group of children are said to be Maureen Elliot and the Browns.

The cathedral from St Oswald's churchyard, 1890s, photographed by F.W. Morgan. The church dates from the late 12th century, but it was partially rebuilt in 1834 by Ignatius Bonomi after damage by mining subsidence. The foundations of an earlier church were confirmed by a dowsing survey carried out in 1983 and supported by an excavation in a small area in the north aisle. The church has an active group which looks after the churchyard memorials and manages the grounds as wildlife conservation areas.

St Oswald's war memorial, Church Street, 13 March 1921, photographed the day it was unveiled. It was dedicated by Bishop Hensley Henson and unveiled by Mrs Roberts of Hollingside, who had lost two sons in the war. The memorial was erected at a cost of £300 in memory of 90 men from the parish who lost their lives during World War One.

The Sun Inn, 34 Hallgarth Street, c.1933, showing the landlord, Mr J.J. Elliott. It is now a private house, appropriately named 'Sun House'. In the 1871 *Walker's Directory* of Durham City, the premises are listed as a Beer House and lived in by Mr J. Robinson, cab proprietor.

The Victoria Hotel, 86 Hallgarth Street, 1920s, taken by Ernest, 21 Silver Street. The landlord, Mr J.W. Marriot, is pictured in the doorway in his shirt sleeves and waistcoat. The gathering seems to include family, friends and customers. This is one of only a handful of watering-holes in the city to have retained its original features. Today a new town house occupies the site of the building on the left of the hotel (separated by Church Lane).

The granary, Elvethall Manor, Hallgarth Street, which belonged to Durham Priory, sketched 'Xmas' 1914 by William George Footitt (1865–1936). This timber-framed building, with cart-shed below, was constructed between 1452–54. On the right is part of the old barn now used as Durham Prison Officers' Club.

The New Inn at the head of Church Street, facing Stockton Road, *c.*1926. Two lads have stopped for an evening drink on the way home after selling all their goods at Durham Market. The inn is marked on John Wood's 1820 map of the city, making it one of the oldest surviving inns. The two cottages on the right were later removed, and a small extension and patio area now occupy their site.

'Mountjoy cut', from the Shincliffe road, 1920s. According to legend, the name 'Mountjoy' is thought to have derived from having been the spot upon which the carriers rested with the body of St Cuthbert, prior to their arrival on the peninsula in AD995. The present road and pathway was later reinforced to support the sandy bank sides.

The street of Whinney Hill, decorated for the visit of King George and Queen Mary to the city, 10 October 1928. The grand entrance was constructed from wood to show off this new council estate. These houses had been built, *c.*1926, to rehouse the occupants of slum dwellings in the New Elvet area.

The ivy-covered house called Newton Wynne (named after the occupant), South End, Elvet, *c.*1900, then the residence of Captain Newton Wynne Apperley, JP, Private Secretary to the Marquess of Londonderry. The building had previously been a coaching inn called The Shepherds' Inn. It is now owned by the university.

CROSSGATE AREA

The ornate shopfront of J.G. Rollin Limited, cash chemist, 3 South Street (left of the Fighting Cocks), *c.*1921. Note the sign above the front door which reads 'cattle medicines'. The shopfrontage was later altered, and the premises were demolished in the 1960s. The present building was recently (October 2006) a branch of Klick photography. The shoppers in the centre are Doretta Richardson, her daughter Sarah and Thomas Thexton.

Mr Alex Gleason, tinsmith, South Street, 1930s. The sign in the window reads 'Pram wheels re tired while you wait'. The shopfrontage and some interior fittings are said to have been salvaged by the Beamish Museum. The site is now occupied by an open area to the right of the Fighting Cocks.

A pencil sketch of the bottom of Crossgate by an unknown artist, showing old business premises, c.1900. On the left is No.73, T.T. Atkinson, hairdresser (note the barber's pole and the small door under the window for coal deliveries to the cellar), and further down is Mrs E. Wilson's confectionary shop. This corner is now occupied by the Halifax Building Society.

Looking up Crossgate, 1940s. The street was originally open for two-way traffic; however, with the advent of motorised transport and the obvious dangers of the steep incline, traffic was later restricted to one way (upwards). The Crossgate Workmen's Club, one of the longest serving in the area, is situated further up the street on the right.

Looking down Crossgate, *c.*1938, taken by W.A. Bramwell. On the right is St Margaret's Church, founded *c.*1150. The sheep were being driven up to the local butcher. The walled entrance to the churchyard behind the railings was later knocked down when the brakes failed on a wagon delivering nearby.

Looking down Neville Street, one of the few remaining cobbled roads left in the city, *c.*1910. St Godric's Church (opened November 1864) can be seen on the skyline. The large building at the bottom on North Road is the former Water Board offices, which is now a bar and restaurant called The Water House and part of the Weatherspoons chain.

The upper part of Crossgate, showing in the centre The Old Elm Tree public house, 1930s. The shop on the left, No. 11½, was Mrs Kirkup's, grocer, and was later converted into a garage and is now back in commercial use as a restaurant attached to a bed and breakfast business.

Old properties above The Old Elm Tree, 1920s. These houses were similar in style to those of New Elvet (see p.105). The buildings were later demolished and the site is now partly occupied by Grape Lane council flats and two detached houses. This stretch of the road still has its granite setts.

A lone policeman directs the traffic at the bottom of Crossgate Peth during the demolition of F. Williamson's butcher and greengrocery shop in 1966. This was the result of a road-widening scheme at Margery Lane. The business was then run by the son, Councillor Norman Williamson. The site is now an open area on the corner occupied by shrubbery.

The shared business premises of J. Waites, horse shoer and general smith, and A. Jopling (joiner undertaker and builder), 26 Crossgate, 1900s. On the left is Jonathan Waites. The property is now converted into a house and let to students, like many in this area.

Three young children in period dress outside the premises of G. Aitcheson's grocers, 1 Alexandria Crescent, c.1905; the street to the left is Crossgate Peth, photographed by W. Wilkinson. These once popular corner shops have now almost disappeared with the coming of the supermarkets and their free car parking.

F. Williamson's butcher and greengrocer, Crossgate Peth, 1960s. Above the door was the inscription Clover Cottage. The property and business had been in the Williamson family since 1899. The corrugated iron extension on the right was the grocery side of the business. The street on the right is Nevilledale Terrace and the one behind the shop is Palatine View (built 1895).

A *Dad's Army*-style van passing the wartime defensive blockade at the bottom of The Avenue, 1939–45. Several of these defences were located around the city. Several years ago archaeologists rediscovered one at Prebends Bridge. The building in the background is part of the former St Margaret's Hospital.

ACTION AFS STATION

Neville's Cross Auxiliary Fire Service crew, with its water-pump, St John's Road, Neville's Cross, August 1941. Third from the left is Tom Curry, who lived locally. A number of these water-pumps were located about the city in case of fire following air raids during World War Two. The building belonged to St John's Church for many years, but it is now converted into a private house.

Durham School, Margery Lane, 1900s, one of the oldest in England, tracing its origins back to mediaeval times. In 1844 it moved here from Palace Green. This area had previously belonged to Bellasis Farm. On the right is the corner block extension of 1887. The gateway on the recent photograph was opened on 30 June 1927 as a memorial to Graham Campbell Kerr, a former pupil and assistant master who became the first civilian Governor of the Sudan.

Looking towards Framwellgate Bridge along the riverside footpath below South Street, 1890s. Note, extreme bottom left, a policeman walking his beat. This path was restored in 1938. This delightful walk ends at Prebends Bridge.

The picturesque Prebends Cottage, 1890s, photographed by F.W. Morgan. It was also once known as 'Bett's Cottage' from the name of a former inhabitant and dates from about the time when Prebends Bridge was built between 1772 and 1778. The road to the right leads to the White Gates, Quarry Heads Lane.

Durham School Chapel during construction, c.1926, taken by John Edis. The chapel was designed by W.H. Brierley and dedicated on 30 September 1926 by Dr Hensley Henson, Bishop of Durham, as a memorial to 97 former boys who had lost their lives in World War One. The names of those killed in World War Two are included on the columns in the nave along with those of World War One.

The old toll house, Potters Bank, 1950s. In 1873, at the monthly meeting of the Durham Board of Health, Councillor T.R. Richardson said 'It was time Durham took some steps to sweep away the whole of the seven toll-gates that barred the free entrance to the city.' The toll-house and adjacent land were sold by auction in 1875 to John Fowler for £70. Today the area is covered with trees and no evidence survives of the former building.

Sledging on the 'Bellas' field (Observatory Hill), *c.*1947, a popular spot in the days when winter seemed whiter. Many locals will remember that when sledging from the top great care had to be taken to avoid the central clump of trees. Recent tree planting and a fence now prevent sledging at the lower end of the slope.

Miss E.M. Spraggon in the garden of Durham Observatory, 1907. Her father was the stationmaster at Sherburn House Station. The observatory was built by Anthony Salvin between 1839–40 for the university, the cost being defrayed by public subscription. The building no longer has telescopes installed and is currently used by the archaeology department.

CLAYPATH AREA

Looking down Claypath, 1943. On the left is Mrs A.H. Pragnell of 70 Claypath collecting her ration of coal after it had been dropped off in the street outside her home. Young boys would take this opportunity to earn a penny or two, by carrying coal from the street into the coalhouse.

No. 48 Claypath, 1885. Notice the stone-slabbed roof and dormer windows before the frontage was heightened. The house appears to be empty and in a neglected state, with its closed ground-floor shutters and obvious signs of rising damp. For a short time this was the residence of the Reverend Alfred Tucker, curate of St Nicholas' Church. He later became the first Bishop of Uganda from 1899–1911.

A rear view of a dwelling on the south side of Claypath, *c.*1926. This old building stood below the Travellers' Rest public house. It is believed to be of a late 17th-century date. The style of the upper dormer windows is a visual sign of their age. The property was later removed in order to enlarge the entrance to the former St Nicholas' vicarage.

Waggott's tobacconist shop, 1 Bluecoat Buildings, Claypath, *c.*1925. The window is filled with pipes, tobacco and walking sticks. The tiled entrance on the left is the former girls' entrance to Bluecoat School. The shop is now occupied by Stuart Edwards, estate agent.

Dancing round the maypole at the May Day celebrations, Bluecoat School, Claypath, c.1963. The event is taking place in front of the caretaker's house, in one of the playgrounds (a garden and access road have now replaced this yard). The school has a history going back to 1708; the foundation stone for the new school at Newton Hall was laid on 6 April 1965. The Claypath site is now occupied by private houses.

Smith the Butcher, 88a Claypath, *c.*1899. The Victorian frontage of this, and the three neighbouring properties on its left, were restored in keeping with the original style in about 1990. Note the worn step of the blocked-up door (now the smaller of the two windows) on the recent photograph. The shop was then vacant (October 2006).

The Maltman Hotel, 29 Claypath, 1960s. On its left is the old Palladium cinema, officially opened on 18 March 1929. The ornate stone archway to the right of the hotel belonged to the Congregational Church and led to the former Presbyterian chapel, built in 1750, still situated behind the present church. The Maltman is now a shop and the old cinema sadly remains empty.

The shopfront of William Wasey, saddler and harness maker, 28 Claypath, 1900s. In the window are an assortment of leather goods; cases, belts, saddles, harnesses, dog collars, whips and much more. It was pulled down to make way for the Palladium cinema (see opposite page). Mr Wasey also had a shop at Blackgate, Coxhoe.

Benny Clark, cycle dealer and repairer, standing in the doorway of 85 Claypath, *c.*1949. Benny, a native of Sherburn Hill, also had a toy stall in Durham Indoor Market. The signs in the window advertise 'Humber Cycles' and the 'Xmas Club'. The premises had previously been occupied by the British Union of Fascists as its Durham office. The shop is now used by a fast food takeaway business called Pizza King.

The Wearmouth Bridge Hotel, 17 Claypath, 1960s. The site is now occupied by council offices and the stage-door entrance lane to the Gala Theatre. On the far left is Adam's confectionary shop; the empty shop window next door was where Norman Richardson opened his first travel agency in 1947. The old City of Durham Gas Company offices on the far right are now a restaurant called Oldfield's.

The lower end of Claypath, *c.*1964. The area in the centre left, beyond the whitewashed first and second-floor frontage, and on the opposite side of the road, was swept away for the road improvements of the 1960s. Bottom left is Dimambros' ice-cream parlour, 90 Claypath. The large building with the dormer window, top right of the old photograph, was the old Co-operative Store.

Looking up Claypath from the lower end, *c.*1910. Middle left is the Grapes Inn, No. 16, showing the landlord's name, Tom Lancaster. In the centre is the spire of the United Reformed Church, built 1885–86 by J.T. Gradon. The properties on the left of the old photograph are now occupied by council offices and a bus stand.

The temporary building belonging to the Co-operative Store, Claypath, August 1967. This was built when the old premises were taken down as part of the redevelopment for the new road scheme. The store later moved to a new building in North Road. The Claypath site is now Millennium Place, opened by HRH Queen Elizabeth II on 8 May 2002 (the author had a display of old photographs that day in Clayport Library).

Ramsbottom, pork butcher, 106 Claypath, *c.*1920, later occupied by Fred Robinson, also a pork butcher. The reflection in the window is of the east side of St Nicholas' Church, which stood opposite. The recent photograph shows the shop window of Next fashion store, part of the Prince Bishops' shopping centre.

The Claypath underpass, June 1967, built to solve Durham's problems by taking vehicles away from its mediaeval streets. The plan for this road was first drawn up in the Sharp report of 1944. The rear of Doggart's department store (now Boots the chemist) stands to the left of the picture. The open space east of the church later became a multi-storey car park. This was demolished to make way for the Prince Bishops' shopping centre (and car park).

Derelict buildings, Paradise Lane area, May 1947. This is now part of the main access road through the city centre. The lower right side of the photograph is now occupied by the slip road leading up from Leazes bowl roundabout towards Claypath. The top of the picture shows the rear of properties in lower Claypath.

Looking up Walkergate (also known as Palace Lane) towards Claypath, 1930s. The signs in the windows of the three-storey building read 'Rooms To Let'. The building at the top of the lane, on the left, was Fleming and Neil, ironmongers. On the right are the steps leading to the Market Place. This ancient right of way is first mentioned in 1283, when William Wickwane, Archbishop of York, fled for his life down these steps to the safety of Kepier Hospital (see *Kepier Hospital* by Dorothy M. Meade (1995)). All the buildings apart from the church hall (top right) were demolished for the Claypath underpass in the 1960s.

Looking down Walkergate towards the Woolpack public house (to the right of the archway), 1870s. This was later (1882) replaced by a building belonging to Henderson's carpet factory then converted into the Palace Theatre (opened in August 1909). On the left is the retaining wall for Durham Indoor Markets. For many years this site was a pleasant open grassed area, sadly sold by the local authority to build expensive apartments (seen under construction in the recent photograph).

The construction of Millburngate Bridge and underpass, March 1966. The bridge was designed by Durham County Council and built by Holst and Company; it was opened on 3 April 1967 by Councillor S.C. Docking JP, Chairman of Durham County Council. In the background Millburngate House is being built. St Godric's Church, on the skyline, seems to be elegantly superior to its new neighbours.

Martin's flour mill, *c.*1933, which was attached to the mediaeval Bishops' Mill (the smaller building on its left). The ice rink was later built on the land at the left-hand side of the old photograph (this is now a bowling alley and fitness centre). The new Millburngate Bridge now crosses the river near this point.

A parade of the Church Lads' Brigade on the Girls' Grammar School playing field near The Sands, 1950s. This pleasant green area is now being developed for new public swimming baths, a decision which has caused much controversy. The buildings behind the spectators belonged to the former Mackays' carpet factory and those on the upper left were on the north side of Claypath. The new apartments on the recent photograph, less than a mile from a World Heritage Site, would be more at home in a Spanish holiday resort.

Buildings belonging to the Durham County Fire Service depot, The Sands, 1950s. Note the brigade's badge on the gable-end; on the right is the scaffolding tower used for training. The Sands is regularly let for the Easter fair and other events. The herbage (i.e. the crop and right of pasture) belongs to the Freemen of the City.

Kepier gatehouse from the riverside, 1920s. The lower doors and windows on the left are now blocked up and the lean-to storage building has long since gone. The road through the archway to Kepier Lane (centre of the photograph) is a public right of way (on foot). The name 'kepier' is made up of two Old English words giving the meaning 'wier with fish trap'.

Kepier farmhouse from the farmyard, 1920s, then lived in by the Harper family (hens and cows roam freely). The old photograph shows the former front door on the right prior to the present porch being built. The land north east of the farm had been scarred by industry (a brickworks and coal mine). The farmer later used this uneven area as an ash tip for the city and charged by the cart-load.

The Kepier gatehouse, built by Richard of Bury, Bishop of Durham from 1333–45, from the farmyard, 1900s, showing a re-enactment from the past. One of the brethren is handing over freshly-caught salmon from the River Wear to the hospital steward. The small outbuilding behind was an ash-closet (toilet). The upper floor of the gatehouse was originally reached by a stone spiral staircase in a turret to the right of the inner arch. When the new entrance and steps were added in the 17th century, the old entrance was used as a coal-house.

Kepier Inn (Kepier Farm), 1880s, showing the landlord's name, John Cuthbertson. This, the former banqueting house of the Heath family, was built in the late 16th century. It was taken down in 1892, leaving only the vaulted ground-floor room and Elizabethan arcade. Recently, the building has undergone restoration to strengthen what remains; the interior has been cleaned out to reveal a fine stone-flagged floor.

GILESGATE AREA

Looking along Gilesgate Moor, in the direction of Belmont, May 1929, photographed by John Edis. On the right is Marshall Terrace and on the left are the front gardens of the newly-built council houses, Kepier Crescent. In the days before supermarkets this was a busy shopping area.

Gilesgate Moor from near the junction with Mill Lane, May 1929, photographed by John Edis. The Grange Foundry public house is partly seen on the extreme left, next to Kepier Crescent. The detached building, centre right, with the gabled frontage, is the Rex cinema, now a tool-hire business. The moor, once part of St Giles parish (now belonging to Belmont), consisted of around 235 acres at the time of its enclosure in 1817.

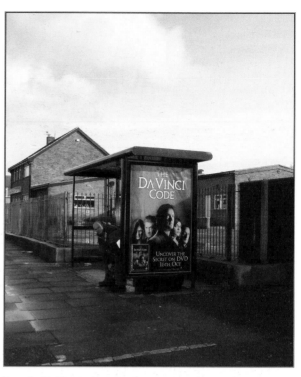

The old Hare and Hounds public house, 39 Sunderland Road, 1960s. Left to right: Tommy Dance, Joe Barker and landlord Matty Cooper. The site is now partly occupied by a bus shelter. To the left of the old photograph can be seen the construction of the new Hare and Hounds, now a veterinary clinic.

A once common street activity at Bells Ville (originally Bell's Villa), Gilesgate Moor, 1950s: Alan and David Routledge are playing marbles. These properties were originally built to house coal miners working in the nearby collieries of Kepier (see p.170) and Old Durham. In the distance are the Kepier Crescent council houses.

The Grange Foundry public house, Gilesgate Moor, showing the landlord, Robert Allison Humble, 1920s. The present building incorporates part of the old premises. The name of the public house derived from the former Grange Iron Works at Carrville, which closed in about 1926. The word grange itself derives from a mediaeval granary and farm belonging to a religious community (e.g. High and Low Grange).

An engraving of Kepier Colliery, Sunderland Road, *c.*1850. The pit was well under way by 1818 and worked the Hutton and Low Main seams, but by 1870 it was unproductive and was abandoned in 1872. The site was later used as a council depot, and the spoil heap from the colliery was levelled and landscaped about 1929 to become the 'Duff Heap', one of the first public playing areas in the city. Several years ago it was regrettably sold by the local authority for housing; at least two of the present houses (on the old council depot) stand on top of one of the old pit shafts. The promise of a replacement play area incorporated into this housing development has yet to be carried out.

Mrs Isabella Fenwick, outside Surprise Cottage, Sherburn Road, 1950s. During World War One she drove a horse-drawn wagon for the North Eastern Railway (at Durham). The building is now the premises of C. Hall, fruit and potato merchant.

Nichol Chilton, fruit and potato merchant, 26 Sherburn Road, c.1914. The business was continued by his son Thomas until the early 1970s. The shop is now converted into a private house. Nichol, a Freeman of the City, was the grandfather of Donald Crampton, who had the successful store in New Elvet.

A view of Sherburn Road from wasteland, prior to the building of Frank Dee's supermarket, 1960s. The gable on the left of the photograph was part of Gibson's general dealers, and the shop over the road is Chilton's (see p.171). The brickwork of the terrace is now hidden behind 1970s-style rendering.

W. Rolling, general dealer, 45a Sunderland Road, *c.*1949. Mr William Rolling's father, George, had started his working life with the Durham Co-operative Store, later branching out by himself with a small shop at 19a Sunderland Road near the present Edge Court. William later took over the concern and had this shop built. The attractive garden is now a car park and the building has lost its character, as the recent photograph shows.

Gilesgate Infants' School, Sunderland Road, 1970s. In its later years it was a well-used youth centre. The lane on the right was once used by a rope maker and is marked on the Ordnance Survey Map of 1877 as a Rope Walk. The school no longer survives. In its place are council bungalows for retired persons.

The old Three Horse Shoes, 16 Sunderland Road, 1920s. The landlord's name (above the door) is Sydney Duncan Curry, although the large faded sign on the front reads 'Matt Henderson, Ale Porter Wine and Spirits'. The small poster in the window advertises Truman's Burton Brewed Bitter. To the right is the passage known as the 'coach opening' after The Railway Coach, the name previously given to the public house (see Ordnance Survey Map of 1877).

The Gilesgate branch of the Annfield Plain Co-operative Society Limited, 1 Sunderland Road, *c*.1967. The area was known locally as the 'store corner'. The buildings on the far left are the rear of Young Street. The recent photograph shows a motorist discount store and raised flower bed occupying the site.

'Sherburn Road Ends' (i.e. the junction of Sunderland and Sherburn Roads), photographed by John Edis, c.1904. On the left is the 'store corner', and on the right is the Queen's Head public house, with the landlord's name, R.E. Coyne, above the door. An ancient site, known as the Maidens' Bower, is marked on old maps as being between Sunderland and Sherburn Roads.

The Gilesgate Church of England School, 1966. It had opened in 1874 (east of the Toll Gate), and so became known as the 'gate school'. It closed in 1932 and, thereafter, was used as St Giles' Parish Hall, but it was demolished in the late 1960s. Part of the original schoolyard wall still survives on the Green Lane side. St Giles' Petrol Station has replaced the former school.

The Bay Horse public house, 110 Gilesgate, 1961, renamed The Durham Light Infantryman in about 1968. The shop on the right had belonged to Jack Reid, cobbler. The posters on the gable advertise 'Cherry Blossom' boot polish. The present building incorporates part of the old pub.

The Militia Barracks (Vane Tempest Hall), 1914–18, taken by John Edis. It was built in 1865 as the 2nd Durham Militia Stores. The postcard shows 'B' Company, Durham Royal Garrison Artillery. Mr G. Etherington, aged 79, wrote some of his memories for *The Durham County Advertiser*, 11 December 1931. He was a former member of the Militia, prior to its moving up to the new barracks. The newspaper recorded: 'Many a good fight was witnessed by him round the Gilesgate 'Duck Pond' when the Militia were at the barracks there, especially when things became lively in the former Canteen Inn' (on the other side of the road, see p.182). The barracks is now occupied by Gilesgate Community Centre.

John Metcalfe outside his premises, 106 Gilesgate, *c.*1925. John was a cartwright and undertaker and traded under his uncle's name of Blenkinsop. The cart in for repair belonged to Dimambros the ice-cream vendors. The man on the right was a debt collector on his rounds. This Grade II listed property was enlarged to the rear and restored in the late 1980s, retaining some of its original character, and is now occupied by Dunelm Veterinary Group.

The Canteen Inn, 97 Gilesgate, *c.*1916, now a private house. It was previously called The Four Alls. The landlord, John R. Beeby, wearing the waistcoat, became landlord of the nearby Bay Horse (now called The Durham Light Infantryman, see p.179) in November 1917. On the right is the Gilesgate Methodist Chapel, now an undertaker's. The recent photograph shows the owner of the former inn, Miss Hilary Webster.

The Duck Pond area, showing the newly-planted avenue of trees, 1890s, photographed by John Edis. The earliest reference to the Duck Pond in St Giles' Church records is dated 1584, when Rycharde Robinson was paid for scouring the 'ducke poole'. It was filled in about 1850 and a horse trough was placed nearby at the top of Gilesgate Bank (south side). This still exists (the only one left in the city), although it has been damaged by recent roadworks.

Three unidentified children photographed at the Duck Pond (Gilesgate Green), September 1952. The recent photograph shows the children presently occupying 128 Gilesgate, Tommy and Spencer Thexton (nephews of the author), and their dog, Tess. The cottages, built in the 1840s, are Grade II listed.

The old office of Wood and Watson Limited, mineral water manufacturers, 132 Gilesgate, c.1960. In the doorway is the owner, Sidney Wood. A new office was built in the 1960s on this site but was taken down (along with the factory behind it) in the 1990s as part of the housing development scheme called St Giles' Close. The present house was designed to blend in with its early 19th-century neighbours on the right. A lane on the left leads down to the Silver Link footbridge (opened in 1938) which crosses the glacial ravine in Pelaw Wood.

The loading bay and stable entrance belonging to Wood and Watsons' 'pop' factory, Gilesgate, c.1925, showing Frank Fowler. In June 1901 a fire had destroyed the old stables then situated to the rear of the factory and only eight of the 20 horses were saved. In the distance is the rounded archway (on the old photograph) leading to the premises of Hayton and Company, wholesale druggist. The recent picture was taken from St Giles' Close.

The garden and rear of 133 Gilesgate, 1900s. On the right is the extension to Wood and Watsons' factory. The pleasant garden was later taken over by the factory to be a covered loading bay. This is now part of a cul-de-sac belonging to St Giles' Close.

On the right is the original site of the Brewers Arms (and George Fowler, brewer), 81 and 82 Gilesgate, 1870s. The property on the left was that of Arthur Thwaites, grocer; the building later became the second home of the Brewers Arms. The building is now converted into student accommodation and is appropriately named 'Brew House'. The property to the right on the recent photograph is a modern inferior building, out of character with the rest of the street.

An old property, once lived in by the then parish clerk of St Giles'
Church, 1900s, which stood opposite the church on the other side of
the road. This humble 17th-century cottage, with its dormer window,
clay pantiled and stone-slabbed roof, was typical of those that would
have lined the street of Gilesgate. Its outline can be seen on the
gable-end of No. 86 Gilesgate. The open space is now the entrance to
an ancient vennel (a north-country term for a narrow lane passing
between houses).

St Giles Church, *c.*1900, from the north side of the road, showing the iron railings that were removed for the war effort by the Ministry of Works in May 1944. The narrow cobbled lane on the right was the original entrance to the church, prior to the creation of the present drive in 1885. The church was founded in 1112 as the hospital chapel of St Giles and became the parish church in about 1180, when the hospital moved to Kepier (see p.165). The recent photograph shows the World War One memorial which was unveiled on 6 May 1925 and records the names of 67 men from the parish.

Looking down Gilesgate Bank from the steep side road, *c.*1904. The bank was cobbled in 1830. About 100 years later the cobbles were replaced with granite setts. These, in turn, were taken up in the early 1960s and a tarmac surface laid. The bank has an ongoing problem with subsidence, due to the sandy condition of the under-surface, along with numerous underground springs.

Salkelds' flying buttress chimney, 173 Gilesgate, 1955. The chimney had become visible from the street when neighbouring properties were demolished in preparation for the new road developments. It was known locally as 'Salkelds' chimney after the occupants. Note the small window in the attic gable and the outline of the former attached property.

The bottom of Gilesgate Bank, 1960s, shortly before the new Leazes Road and the roundabout were built. The central gable-fronted building is the Volunteer Arms public house, and the large building a little to its left is the old drill hall of the 8th Battalion Durham Light Infantry. The properties in the distance (on the old photograph) are the lower end of Gilesgate, near the Woodman Inn.

Looking down Station Lane, towards the bottom of Gilesgate Bank, 1930s. A young boy is seen loading his sack-barrow with bags of coal from the nearby Kiplings' coalyard. It was here, at No. 4 Station Lane, that World War One, Victoria Cross hero Michael Heaviside was born on 28 October 1880.

Gilesgate Goods Station from the 'engine bridge', 1950s. The station was opened in 1844 for goods traffic (April) and passengers (June). After 1857, when the present North Road station opened, it was goods only, finally closing on 7 November 1966. It had a single branch line two-and-a-half-miles long, joining the Leamsine line at Carrville. This is now the A690 road.

Gilesgate Goods Station, showing the enquiry office, waiting rooms and fair-sized station master's house (extreme right), situated on the north-west side of the station, photographed in the 1960s. It was designed by G.T. Andrews of York (the architect of York Station) and opened in 1844. The central arched doorway is now the guest entrance to the Travelodge (facing the A690).

The doors of the engine shed, belonging to Gilesgate Goods Station, 1962. The shed later became Archibald's hardware store. It is now a restaurant and the foreground is a car park. Since the demolition of the lower end of Station Lane (see p.195) fine views can be seen of the city.

The lower end of Gilesgate in the snow, 1938, looking across the road towards the Woodman Inn, photographed by Danny Webster. A snowplough fights its way through the snow-covered street, followed by many workers armed with shovels, drafted from the ranks of the unemployed.

Mr Robert Robertson outside the Woodman Inn, 23 Gilesgate, 1920s. This early 18th-century inn was demolished and later rebuilt. The old front-door lintel, carved 'GM. 1715', was salvaged and placed above a rear door of the new inn. The property had at one time belonged to the Gillygate Church Estate Charity.

The premises of R.J. Maddison, general dealer, 201 Gilesgate, 1880s, photographed by Obadiah Woodcock of 193 Gilesgate. Maddison, a Freeman of the city, first started his business in Claypath, later moving to this address. The trapdoor in the pavement (on the left) led to the cellar. The left door on the old photograph is now the front door of the present house.

Two recently built houses in Mayorswell Close, Gilesgate, 1930s. Note the old gas lamp with resting bracket for the lamplighter's ladder (see p.69). The name Mayorswell is likely to have come from the name of a family called Maire who had property in this area in the 17th century. (Like many city streets, this area is now becoming a students' quarter.)

Mayors' Well Street (built in 1878), Gilesgate, 1930s, situated in the area behind the Woodman Inn. The unkept road at the front of the houses has now been divided into small gardens; the recent photograph shows overgrown hedges obscuring the frontage of the street.

The band and men of the 8th Battalion Durham Light Infantry, marching towards Claypath from their drill hall (see p.194), *c.*1908. Their appearance suggests a Sunday morning church parade as the street seems to be relatively empty. The houses on the north side of the street have changed very little over the last 100 years.

The Chains, Gilesgate, from the Claypath end of the street, c.1900, photographed by T.W. Salkeld. The house on the left was a tenement property known locally as 'Jacob's Ladder'. Council flats, called The Chains, were later built (set back from the road) in the 1950s. The area is named after the chain-horses which operated from this stretch of road, helping heavy horse-drawn wagons up and down Claypath.

Looking down Ravensworth Terrace (built in the 1880s, opposite The Chains), *c.*1946. The short street on the left, at its foot, was Pelaw Terrace (demolished for the new road in the mid-1960s). Because of the steepness of this hill, a handrail was specially installed to help people up and down.

Bakehouse Lane, *c.*1933, part of the ancient
boundary between St Nicholas' and St Giles'
parishes. The name derived from the communal
bakehouse which stood nearby. On the right is the
gable-end of the former General Gordon public
house, now a private residence. The property on the
left (see p.205) was later removed and the lane
widened as an access road. On the bottom right of
both photographs is one of three curved stones
('skiffs') which were designed to prevent damage to
the wall by cartwheels.

Woodbine Cottage, on the north side of the river near Baths Bridge, *c.*1964. This gracious Georgian house had to be taken down after a landslide during the construction of the Leazes Road caused structural damage. Many will remember the little sweet shop attached to the house at the bottom of Tinkler's Lane.